GREET MOMENTS IN
WORLD CUP HISTORY

•

JOHN S. SNYDER

•

C H R O N I C L E   B O O K S
SAN FRANCISCO

Printed in Singapore.

ISBN 0-8118-0463-1

Library of Congress Cataloging-in-Publication Data available.

Design by T·H Typecast, Inc.
Cover and interior illustration by Charlie Powell
Cover design by Joe Stitzlein

Distributed in Canada by Raincoast Books,
112 East Third Avenue, Vancouver, B.C. V5T 1C8

10 9 8 7 6 5 4 3 2

Chronicle Books
275 Fifth Street
San Francisco, CA 94103

INTRODUCTION

FOR MORE THAN 500 million players and billions of addicts who call themselves fans, the World Cup is the most important athletic competition on earth. Its importance combines the history and tradition of the World Series, the spectacle of the Super Bowl, the nationalistic fervor of the Olympics, and the pursuit of the Holy Grail.

The World Cup tournament has taken place every four years since 1930, except for 1942, when the Second World War prevented play, and 1946, when most of the global nations were still recovering from the war.

Governed by the Federation Internationale de Football Association (FIFA), the

World Cup began as
a modest event with 13 countries entering. In 1990, 112 nations
played in the qualifying round for the coveted
24 spots in the final round.

The number of teams in the final round has var-
ied: there were 16 from 1954 through 1978, and 24
since 1982. All but two of the 24 teams have to qualify
through a grueling set of international matches that
begin more than two years before the finals. The defending champion and the host nation are automati-
cally in the final round.

The format for the final round has been
changed several times, but has been the same
since 1986. The 24 teams are divided
into six groups of four. Each
team plays every

team in its group once, a total of three games. The top two teams with the best records in each group advance to the second round, along with the four third-place teams with the best record. These 16 survivors are seeded into a knockout (lose one game and you're out) tournament. Ultimately, two teams compete for the championship, and the two losers in the semifinal matches play an additional game to determine third place.

Only six nations have claimed the World Cup championship: Brazil, Italy, and West Germany three times each; Uruguay and Argentina twice; and England once. Geography has played an important part in determining the champion. One country serves as host for each

World Cup, and matches are held in several of its cities and towns. The host nation has won five of the 14 tournaments. Brazil, in 1958, is the only nation to win after crossing an ocean. European teams have won all of the other tournaments on European soil and South American teams have won all of the World Cups played in South or North America.

Goal! recaptures the amazing feats and unbroken records in World Cup history and brings to life the exciting and often forgotten stories behind the statistics.

All of the records in the book are for the final round through the 1990 tournament, unless otherwise indicated.

RAIMUNDO ORSI

THE PLAYER WHO kicked a fluke goal to help Italy win the 1934 World Cup final.

Italy was in desperate straits in the 1934 World Cup final against Czechoslovakia in Rome. The Italians trailed 1-0 with eight minutes to play when Raimundo Orsi took a pass from Enrique Guaita, ran through the Czech defense, feinted with his left foot, and shot with his right. The ball swerved crazily, brushed goalkeeper Frantisek Plánička's fingers, and curled into the net. Italy went on to win 2-1 in extra time. The next day, Orsi tried to repeat the feat for photographers but was unsuccessful on 20 attempts, even without a goalkeeper to stop him.

1

TEÓFILO CUBILLAS

THE ONLY PLAYER to score at least five goals in two different World Cup tournaments.

Starring for Peru, Teófilo Cubillas had five goals in 1970 and five more in 1978. He is tied for fifth all-time in total goals scored and may have had a shot at the record of 14 goals had Peru qualified for the final round in 1974 or advanced beyond the quarterfinals in 1970 or 1978. Cubillas had his 10 goals in just eight games. He was at his best on June 3, 1978, when he scored two goals and set up another in a 3-1 win over Scotland in Córdoba, Argentina. Cubillas scored three times against Iran on June 11, 1978, as Peru won 4-1.

2

COLOMBIA

THE TEAM THAT stunned the USSR with a 4-4 draw in 1962.

The USSR figured to have no trouble with Colombia on June 3, 1962, in Arica, Chile, as Colombia had never earned a point in final-round competition. The Soviets led 3-0 after 11 minutes and 4-1 after 10 minutes of the second half. With one of the world's best goalkeepers in Lev Yashin, the USSR seemed assured of a win. But the Colombians struck with three goals in 10 minutes to come away with a stunning 4-4 tie, which proved to be the surprise of the 1962 tournament.

ZBIGNIEW BONIEK

THE ONLY POLISH star to score on a
header, a pass, and a dribble in one match.

Zbigniew Boniek was spectacular for Poland on
June 28, 1982, against Belgium in Barcelona, Spain.
He scored on a pass in the fourth minute, headed a goal
in the 26th, and scored off a dribble in the 53rd to pro-
vide all of the game's goals in a 3-0 win. Boniek also
played for Poland in 1978 and 1986 and has six career
World Cup goals.

ITALY VS.
CZECHOSLOVAKIA, 1934

THE FIRST WORLD Cup final to go into extra time.

Three of the 14 finals have gone into extra time. The first was between Italy and Czechoslovakia on June 10, 1934, in Rome. The game was scoreless for 70 minutes before Antonin Puč of Czechoslovakia shot the ball past Italian goalkeeper Giampiero Combi. With eight minutes left in regulation, Italy tied the score at 1-1 when Raimundo Orsi shot over Czech keeper Frantisek Plánička. Play went into extra time, where the only goal was scored by Angelo Schiavio in the 95th minute. Italy had a 2-1 win and the championship.

GERD MÜLLER

THE PLAYER WHO scored the most
World Cup goals in a career.

Gerd Müller of West Germany is the all-time leading goal scorer in Cup history with 14. Known for his
explosive shot and uncanny sense of positioning, Müller
scored 10 goals in 1970 and four in 1974. In 1970 in
Mexico, he twice scored three goals in a game, once in a
5-2 triumph over Bulgaria, and a second time in a 3-1
victory over Peru. In 1974, Müller helped West
Germany win the World Cup with one goal in four
different contests, including a 2-1 win over
Netherlands in the final.

6

PETER RADAKOVIĆ

THE PLAYER WHO scored the goal that
put Yugoslavia into the semifinals for the
only time in its history.

Yugoslavia had lost to West Germany in the quarterfinals in both 1954 and 1958, and had to face them again
in the quarters on June 10, 1962, in Santiago, Chile.
Yugoslavia won this time 1-0 to advance to the semifinals for the only time in its history. The goal was scored
in the 87th minute by Peter Radaković, who had his
head wrapped in bandages from an injury suffered
earlier in the game. Yugoslavia lost in the semis
1-0 to host Chile.

SPAIN

THE HOST NATION that scheduled matches in 17 different stadiums.

Spain set a record as host in 1982 by using 17 different stadiums in 14 cities and towns to play the 52 World Cup final-round contests. The games were played in Madrid, Barcelona, Alicante, Seville, Málaga, Valencia, Zaragoza, Bilbao, Vallidolid, Elche, Gijón, Oviedo, Vigo, and La Coruña. Two different stadiums were used in Madrid, Barcelona, and Seville.

BRYAN ROBSON

THE PLAYER WHO scored the quickest goal in World Cup history.

Bryan Robson of England scored the quickest World Cup goal in history after just 27 seconds of play in a 3-1 win over France on June 16, 1982, in Bilbao, Spain. It was the first match of the tournament for both teams, and Robson scored again later in the match. It was also the first time Robson played in a World Cup game in the final round.

9

ANTONIO CARBAJAL

THE ONLY PLAYER to appear in five
final rounds.

Antonio Carbajal played goalkeeper for Mexico in
the final round a record five times, appearing in 1950,
1954, 1958, 1962, and 1966. He played in 11 games in
all. In those contests, Mexico had a record of just one
win, eight defeats, and two draws. The lone win came on
June 7, 1962, Carbajal's 33rd birthday, as Mexico beat
Czechoslovakia 3-1. It is also Mexico's only victory in
a final-round game on foreign soil.

POLAND

THE COUNTRY THAT did not win a
World Cup game before 1974, but has won
13 since.

Poland came out of nowhere to win Olympic gold in
1972 and finish third in the World Cup tournament in
both 1974 and 1978. Poland qualified for the World
Cup in 1938, but did not reach the final round again
until 1974. That year, Poland had six wins in seven
games to finish in third place. Poland followed up
with final-round appearances in 1978, 1982, and
1986, and with another third-place finish in
1986. Its overall record is 13 wins, seven
losses, and five ties.

BRAZIL

THE TEAM THAT benched two star players in the 1938 semifinals to rest them for the final.

Brazil was so confident of victory in the 1938 semifinal against Italy on June 16 in Marseilles, France, that it rested Leónidas and Tim, two of its star players, so they would be fresh in the final. Brazil also brazenly booked the only available plane to Paris, where the final would be played, and made no provisions for travel to Bordeaux for the third-place game, which would be their fate should they lose. Defending champion Italy won 2-1, with Brazil's only goal a meaningless one in the 87th minute.

ANGELO SCHIAVIO

THE FIRST PLAYER to score an extra-time goal in a World Cup final.

With the score 1-1 between Italy and Czecho-slovakia in the 95th minute of the 1934 World Cup final, Angelo Schiavio of Italy produced the first extra-time goal in a final to give the Italians a 2-1 triumph. Schiavio took a pass from Enrique Guaita and beat a Czech defender before shooting past goalkeeper Frantisek Plánička.

EDWARD BETCHLEY

THE THIEF WHO stole the World Cup trophy in 1966.

Scotland Yard sprang into action on March 20, 1966, when the trophy was stolen from Central Hall, Westminster. It had been brought to England from Brazil to be displayed in advance of the World Cup being played in July. The trophy was discovered a few days later by a mongrel dog named Pickles. Pickles was digging for a bone in the backyard of his owner's London home and instead unearthed the Cup. Police tracked the crime to Edward Betchley, who stole the Cup to hold it for ransom.

Pickles became a national hero.

CAMEROON

THE FIRST AFRICAN team to reach the quarterfinals.

The 1990 Cameroon team was the first African squad from south of the Sahara Desert to win a World Cup match and the first from anywhere on the continent to reach the quarterfinals. Cameroon stunned defending champion Argentina in the opening game 1-0 on June 8 in Milan, Italy. The only goal was scored by Omam Biyik in the 66th minute. Cameroon played 26 minutes with 10 players and the last four with nine, but held off the Argentines. Cameroon won three and lost two in the tournament.

The quarterfinal loss was to England by a 3-2 score.

15

ANTON SCHALL

THE FIRST PLAYER to score an extra-
time goal in World Cup history.

Anton Schall of Austria scored the first extra-time
goal in World Cup history on May 27, 1934, against
France in Turin, Italy. Schall's goal broke a 1-1 tie in
Austria's 3-2 victory. Most observers thought Schall was
obviously offside. Years later, Schall admitted that he
probably was.

NEW ZEALAND

THE TEAM TO score the most goals in one game in a qualifying round.

New Zealand set the all-time World Cup record for goal scoring in a game in a qualifying-round match against Fiji on August 16, 1981, in Auckland, New Zealand, which the New Zealanders won 13-0. Steve Sumner scored six goals. The win helped New Zealand qualify for the final round in 1982, for the only time in its history. New Zealand lost all three games in the tournament, played in Spain, falling 5-2 to Scotland, 3-0 to the USSR, and 4-0 to Brazil.

JUAN HOHBERG

THE PLAYER WHO was knocked out
by his own teammates after scoring a goal in
1954.

Juan Hohberg of Uruguay scored a goal with four minutes remaining to tie Hungary 2-2 in the semifinals on
June 30, 1954, in Lausanne, Switzerland, and his teammates knocked him out cold when they rushed en masse
to celebrate. Hohberg recovered and hit the post with a
shot in extra time, but Uruguay lost 4-2.

18

EGYPT

THE FIRST TEAM from Africa to play
in the final round of the World Cup.

The 1934 Egyptian national team was the first
from Africa to play in a World Cup final-round game.
Egypt played only one game in the tournament and lost
4-2 to Hungary on May 27 in Naples, Italy. Egypt did
not play in the final round again until 1990, when it
played three matches with a defeat and two draws.

THE WALTERS
AND THE CHARLTONS

THE TWO PAIRS of brothers who played together on World Cup championship teams.

The first brothers to play together on a championship team in World Cup play were Fritz and Ottmar Walter of West Germany in 1954. The second pair were Bobby and Jack Charlton with England in 1966.

LUÍS MONTI

THE ONLY INDIVIDUAL to play in a World Cup final for two different nations.

Taking advantage of an Italian law which stated that Argentines could have dual citizenship, Luís Monti played for his native Argentina in the 1930 World Cup final and for champion Italy in 1934. Three others have played in the final round for two different countries. They are José Altafini (Brazil in 1958, when he was known as Mazzola, and Italy in 1962), Ferenc Puskás (Hungary in 1954 and Spain in 1962), and José Santamaria (Uruguay in 1954 and Spain in 1962).

BERNE, SWITZERLAND

THE SMALLEST CITY to host a World Cup final.

The fifth World Cup final was played in Berne, Switzerland, on July 4, 1954, in Wankdorf Stadium and resulted in a 3-2 win by West Germany over Hungary. Berne, which then had a population of about 150,000, is the smallest city ever to host a World Cup final. The 1954 World Cup was the first to be shown on television.

WEST GERMANY VS.
ARGENTINA, 1990

THE LOWEST-SCORING World Cup final.

The 1990 final between West Germany and Argentina on July 8, 1990, in Rome was the lowest-scoring final in history, and the only occasion in which the same two teams met in the final in successive World Cups. West Germany beat Argentina 1-0 after Argentina had beaten the West Germans 3-2 in 1986. The 1990 final was scoreless until Rudi Völler of West Germany was downed by Argentina's Roberto Sensini in the penalty area. A penalty kick was awarded to West Germany, and Andreas Brehme converted to give West Germany its third championship.

TURKEY

THE ONLY NATION to average more
than three goals per game in World Cup play.

Amazingly, Turkey holds the record for the highest
goals-per-game average, all-time, in World Cup play.
The only year the team qualified was in 1954 in
Switzerland, and the Turks scored 10 times in three
games for an average 3.33 goals per match. But Turkey
was outscored 11-10 and lost two of three. It lost 4-1
and 7-2 in two matches against West Germany and
defeated South Korea 7-0.

NORTH KOREA

THE NATION THAT stunned Italy in
1966 in its only appearance in the World Cup
final round.

North Korea has reached the final round of the World
Cup only once, but made quite an impression. The
North Koreans opened with a 3-0 loss to the USSR, but
tied Chile 1-1 and stunned heavily favored Italy 1-0 to
pull off one of the greatest upsets in World Cup history. The lone goal was scored by Pak Doo Ik in the
42nd minute. It was the first time a team from
Asia won a World Cup game. The victory
allowed North Korea to reach the quarterfinals, where it led Portugal 3-0
before falling 5-3.

ERNIE BRANDTS

THE PLAYER WHO scored for each team and injured his own goalkeeper in the same game.

The Netherlands needed a win or a draw against Italy on June 21, 1978, in Buenos Aires in order to reach the final. Eighteen minutes into the game, Ernie Brandts of the Netherlands kicked savagely at the ball in front of his own goal, knocked the ball into the netting, and crippled teammate goalkeeper Pieter Schrijvers, who was carried off on a stretcher. Brandts recovered from the embarrassment, and five minutes into the second half, he scored on a free kick. The Netherlands went on to win 2-1.

VICENTE FEOLA

THE TEAM MANAGER who delayed his
return home for a month after losing the
World Cup.

Vicente Feola was manager of Brazil's World Cup
champions in 1958. Illness prevented him from direct-
ing the team in 1962, as the Brazilians won again, but
Feola returned as manager in 1966. Playing in England,
Brazil opened the 1966 tournament with a 2-0 win over
Bulgaria, but lost 3-1 to Hungary and 3-1 again
against Portugal. There was so much outrage in
Brazil over the team's poor performance that
Feola stayed in Europe for a month before
returning home.

27

LUXEMBOURG

THE ONLY NATION to lose 32 consecutive qualifying matches.

The Grand Duchy of Luxembourg, a country of
360,000 people, has to be given credit for trying. Its
national soccer team has entered every World Cup
qualifying round since 1934 despite a long string of
failures. Luxembourg's qualifying record through 1990
is two wins, one draw, and 63 defeats with 37 goals
scored and 241 against. It lost 32 in a row between
1974 and 1990. The wins were over Portugal by a
4-2 count in 1962 and against Turkey by a 2-0
score in 1974. In 1990, Luxembourg tied
Belgium 1-1 to end the 32-match
losing streak.

JORGE BURRUCHAGA

THE PLAYER WHO scored the winning
goal with seven minutes remaining in the
1986 final.

Argentina and West Germany were the opponents
for the World Cup final on June 29, 1986, in Mexico
City. Argentina took a 2-0 lead on goals in the 22nd and
55th minutes. The team could not hold off a West
German rally, however, which produced goals in the
73rd and 81st minutes. In the 83rd minute, Jorge
Burruchaga of Argentina took a perfect pass and
ran half the length of the field to beat West
German goalkeeper Harald Schumacher.
Argentina had a thrilling 3-2 win
and the championship.

MARIO DE LAS CASAS

THE FIRST PLAYER to be ejected from
a World Cup match.

Peru's captain Mario De Las Casas has the distinc-
tion of being the first player to be ejected from a World
Cup match. It happened on July 14, 1930, in Peru's 3-1
loss to Romania. De Las Casas was sent off by referee
Alberto Warken of Chile for progressively violent play.

HUNGARY

THE TEAM THAT scored the most goals in a final-round game.

Hungary set the record for most goals scored in a final-round game on June 15, 1982, in a 10-1 win over El Salvador in Elche, Spain. Hungary led 3-0 at the half, then scored seven after intermission against El Salvador. It was Hungary's only win of the tournament. The Hungarians lost 4-1 to Argentina on June 18 and tied Belgium 1-1 on June 22.

SPAIN VS. ITALY, 1934

THE FIRST WORLD Cup match to be replayed entirely.

In many of the early World Cup tournaments, games that remained tied after 120 minutes were re-played in their entirety. There have been four in World Cup history, with one in 1934 and three in 1938. The first was played between Spain and Italy in the quarterfi-nals on June 1, 1934, in Florence, Italy. The day before, the two teams had battled to a 1-1 tie after 90 minutes of regulation play and 30 minutes of extra time. In the replay, Italy won 1-0.

KHEMAIS LABIDI AND
MARCELO TROBBIANI

THE TWO PLAYERS who share the
record for the shortest career in World Cup
final-round competition.

Khemais Labidi of Tunisia and Marcelo Trobbiani of
Argentina share the record for the shortest World Cup
final-round career at two minutes. Labidi played the last
two minutes of a match against Mexico on June 2, 1978,
in Rosario, Argentina, which Tunisia won 3-1.
Trobbiani played the final two minutes of the 1986
final for his only World Cup appearance on June 29
in Mexico City as Argentina downed West
Germany 3-2.

ENGLAND VS. BRAZIL

THE MUCH-ANTICIPATED match in
1970 pairing the winners of the previous
three World Cups.

When the pairings were announced for the 1970
World Cup in Mexico, the match between England,
champions of 1966, and Brazil, victors in 1958 and
1962, was the match everyone circled on their calendars.
The teams met on June 7 in Guadalajara in group play.
In the first half, English goalkeeper Gordon Banks
made an unbelievable save of a Pelé header, as
Banks twisted backward and up to scoop the
ball over the crossbar. Banks could not
stop a shot by Jairhinzo, however,
and Brazil won 1-0.

34

JEAN LANGENUS

THE REFEREE WHO settled a controversy over the use of a ball during the first
World Cup final.

Jean Langenus of Belgium refereed the first World Cup
final, between Uruguay and Argentina, on July 30,
1930, in Montevideo, Uruguay. A controversy erupted
because each team wanted to use its own ball for play.
Langenus decreed that each ball would be used for one
half. Argentina won the coin toss and elected to use its
ball for the first half. Uruguay scored first, but
Argentina took a 2-1 lead. Uruguay had its ball
in the second half and reached goal three
times for a 4-2 win.

LASZLO KISS

THE ONLY SUBSTITUTE to score three goals in a game.

Laszlo Kiss of Hungary played only the final 34 minutes against El Salvador on June 15, 1982, in Elche, Spain, but found time to become the only substitute in World Cup history to score three goals in a game. Hungary won in a 10-1 rout.

EUSÉBIO

THE PLAYER WHO led all scorers in 1966 with nine goals for Portugal.

Playing for Portugal, Mozambique-born Eusébio (Eusébio da Silva Ferreira) led all scorers with nine goals in the 1966 World Cup in England. Explosive and entertaining, Eusébio could dribble with lightning speed through a densely packed defense. He scored three goals in the first three games to help Portugal win all three and advance to the quarterfinals, where he had his greatest moment. Portugal trailed North Korea 3-0 when Eusébio retaliated with four goals and set up a fifth for a 5-3 win.

MONTEVIDEO, URUGUAY

THE ONLY CITY to host an entire World Cup tournament.

Uruguay successfully lobbied to become the host of the first World Cup in 1930. All of the games were played in Montevideo, then a city with a population of about 480,000. It is the only city to host an entire tournament, although the games were played at three different stadiums. The final was played in the just-completed Centenary Stadium, where Uruguay defeated Argentina 4-2. Subsequent World Cups were hosted by one country, but the games were played in several different cities and towns.

DENMARK

THE NATION THAT made its World
Cup debut in 1986 and won its first three
matches.

Denmark did not reach the final round of the World
Cup until 1986, then stunned everyone by winning its
first three games. A small nation whose best players
made their living professionally in other countries,
Denmark beat Scotland 1-0, Uruguay 6-1, and West
Germany 2-0 before losing to Spain 5-1. Denmark did
not qualify in 1990, falling only a point shy in a
four-team group behind Romania.

ARGENTINA

THE ONLY NATION to reach the semifinals at least four times without a defeat.

Argentina has won all four times it has reached the
semis of a World Cup tournament, with victories in
1930, 1978, 1986, and 1990. Argentina won the championship in 1978 and 1986. The nation has won 24
games in the final round, the fourth highest total in Cup
history, even though the Argentines did not enter the
tournament in 1938, 1950, and 1954. Argentina has
qualified for the final round every year it has
entered except 1970. Since 1978, its World
Cup record is 15 wins, six losses, and
five draws.

PORTUGAL

THE WORLD CUP team that voted to
go on strike in 1986.

Angered by the refusal of team officials to double
their tournament bonuses, Portugal's 1986 World Cup
team decided to go on strike and boycott training ses-
sions through the start of the tournament. President
Mario Soares sent a telegram appealing to officials and
players to resolve their differences. One day later, the
players abandoned their boycott. Once play began,
Portugal surprised England with a 1-0 win in the
opener, but lost its other two matches, 1-0 to
Poland and 3-1 to Morocco.

1982 WORLD CUP

THE FIRST WORLD Cup with 24 teams in the final round.

João Havelange of Brazil was elected president of the FIFA in 1974 with the promise that he would expand the World Cup final field from 16 nations to 24 in order to allow more teams from Asia, Africa, and Central and North America to compete. The move was widely criticized in Europe and South America, but Havelange was vindicated when teams from Cameroon, Algeria, Kuwait, and Honduras pulled off magnificent surprises in the 1982 tournament and provided exciting play.

ITALY

THE TEAM THAT changed its flight
plans home from the 1966 World Cup to
avoid its fans.

Italy was expected to field a strong star-filled World
Cup team in 1966 in England, but won only one game
and lost two, including a shocking 1-0 loss to North
Korea. Frightened by the negative reaction of their coun-
trymen, the Italian team jettisoned a plan to return to
Rome in midday, and instead routed the team plane to
Genoa in the middle of the night. The ruse did not
work, however, as the players were greeted by a
barrage of rotten vegetables, many of which
were better aimed than the team's
shots on goal had been.

43

SANDOR KOCSIS

THE ONLY PLAYER to score seven goals
in back-to-back World Cup matches.

Perhaps the greatest header of the ball in soccer history, Sandor Kocsis of Hungary scored seven goals in
back-to-back games at the 1954 World Cup in
Switzerland. Playing inside right, Kocsis scored three
goals in Hungary's opening game, a 9-0 rout of South
Korea on June 17. Three days later, he added four goals
in an 8-3 triumph over West Germany. Kocsis scored
11 goals altogether in the tournament, netting two
against Brazil, a 4-2 win, and two in a 4-2
semifinal victory over Uruguay.

LUCIEN LAURENT

THE FIRST PLAYER to score a goal in
World Cup competition.

Lucien Laurent of France became the first World
Cup scorer on the eve of Bastille Day, July 13, 1930, in
a 4-1 win over Mexico in Montevideo, Uruguay. It came
19 minutes into the match on a powerful shot that went
by Mexican goalkeeper Oscar Bonfiglio. It was the only
World Cup goal of Laurent's career.

JOSÉ BATISTA

THE ONLY PLAYER to be ejected from
a World Cup match before one minute of
play had elapsed.

José Batista of Uruguay did not last long in a match
against Scotland on June 13, 1986, in Toluca, Mexico.
He was ejected just 55 seconds into the game for rough
play. The game ended in a 0-0 tie.

GARY LINEKER

THE PLAYER WHO led all scorers in a
World Cup by netting six of his team's seven
goals.

Gary Lineker of England led all scorers at the 1986
World Cup in Mexico with six of his team's seven
goals. The entire English team was shut out in the first
two games of the tournament, a 1-0 loss to Portugal and
a scoreless draw with Morocco, but Lineker broke free
in the third contest by scoring all three goals in a 3-0
win over Poland. He added two more as England
advanced with a 3-0 triumph over Paraguay
and netted a goal against Argentina in
the quarterfinals, although England
lost 2-1.

URUGUAY VS.
ARGENTINA, 1930

THE ONLY WORLD Cup final to match
the gold and silver medalists from the previous Olympics.

Uruguay defeated Argentina 2-1 in the 1928 Olympic
gold-medal soccer match, and the two border rivals
met again in the first World Cup final on July 30, 1930,
in Montevideo. Thousands of Argentine fans poured
across the Río de la Plata, which separated the two
countries, to swell the crowd to 90,000. Amid tight
security, Uruguay claimed the World Cup with a
4-2 victory.

48

FRANCE

THE FIRST HOST nation to fail to win a World Cup championship.

Host nations Uruguay in 1930 and Italy in 1934 won the first two World Cups, but France in 1938 failed to keep the streak alive as Italy won again. The 1938 French team beat Belgium 3-1 and lost to Italy 3-1. Other host nations to win were England in 1966, West Germany in 1974, and Argentina in 1978.

49

NEPAL

THE NATION TO allow the most unanswered goals during a qualifying round.

The record for most goals allowed without scoring in a qualifying round is held by Nepal in 1990 when it lost six matches by an aggregate score of 28-0. Nepal first entered World Cup competition in 1986 qualifying and was outscored 11-0 in four games, but it did manage a 0-0 tie with Malaysia.

ITALY

THE ONLY WORLD Cup champion to fail to win a match until its fourth game of the tournament.

Italy won the World Cup in 1982 for the third time in its history, led on the field by Paolo Rossi and 40-year-old goalkeeper Dino Zoff. In group play, Italy played to three draws, against Poland, Peru, and Cameroon. Italy advanced to the second round only because it had scored two goals while Cameroon had scored just once, also in three draws. Italy beat Argentina 2-1 and Brazil 3-2 in the second round, and took Poland 2-0 in the semifinals. Italy took the Cup with a 3-1 win over West Germany.

51

ERNST WILLIMOWSKI

THE ONLY PLAYER to score four goals
in one game in a losing effort.

Ernst Willimowski of Poland scored four goals
against Brazil from his inside forward position on June
5, 1938, in Strasbourg, France, but Poland lost 6-5 as
Leónidas scored four goals for the Brazilians. Willimowski's four-goal performance came in the first round
and proved to be the only World Cup final-round game
of his career.

RAJKO MITIĆ

THE PLAYER WHO missed the start of
a 1950 match because he cut his head on a
girder.

Rajko Mitić of Yugoslavia was walking toward the
field from the locker room underneath massive
Maracana Stadium in Rio de Janeiro for a match against
Brazil on July 1, 1950, when he hit his head on a girder,
causing a severe cut on his forehead. At the time, substitutions were not allowed, so the Yugoslavians had
to choose whether to play at full strength without
Mitić or to start with 10 players while Mitić
was being stitched up. Yugoslavia started
a man short, and Mitić played later,
but Brazil won 2-0.

53

ALFRED BICKEL
AND ERIK NILSSON

THE ONLY TWO players to participate in the final round both before and after World War II.

Alfred Bickel of Switzerland and Erik Nilsson of Sweden are the only two players to participate in the final round of the World Cup before and after World War II. Both played in 1938 and 1950.

JUAN BASAGUREN

THE FIRST SUBSTITUTE to score in a World Cup.

Juan Basaguren of Mexico made history on June 7, 1970, against El Salvador in Mexico City by becoming the first substitute to replace a substitute and the first substitute to score a goal. Basaguren scored seven minutes before time in Mexico's 4-0 win. Basaguren was also a substitute in a June 11 contest versus Belgium.

FRANCE VS.
WEST GERMANY, 1982

THE FIRST WORLD Cup match to end
on penalty kicks.

West Germany defeated France in the most dra-
matic semifinal in World Cup history on July 8, 1982,
in Seville, Spain. After 90 minutes, the score was 1-1.
France exploded in extra time with two goals. Karl-
Heinz Rummenigge of West Germany scored to make it
3-2 France. With two minutes remaining, Klaus Fischer
scored for West Germany to tie 3-3. For the first time,
a World Cup match was decided on penalties. West
Germany converted five of six shots to France's
four to advance to the final.

HUNGARY

THE NATION WHOSE only defeat in international play between 1950 and 1956 came in the 1954 World Cup final.

Hungary dominated international competition during the early 1950s. From May 1950 through June 1956, Hungary won 47 of 48 international matches. Unfortunately, this great team did not win the World Cup. Hungary did not enter the 1950 competition, and the lone defeat in Hungary's remarkable six-year run of domination came in the 1954 World Cup final, a stunning 3-2 upset at the hands of West Germany.

DUTCH EAST INDIES

THE FIRST TEAM from Asia to play in
the World Cup.

The Dutch East Indies (today known as Indonesia)
qualified for the World Cup final round in 1938 as the
first team ever from Asia. The team made the long jour-
ney to France, to play just one game, a 6-0 loss to
Hungary on June 5 in Reims. It is the only World Cup
final-round game in the country's history.

MEXICO

THE ONLY NATION to lose more than 15 final-round games.

Mexico has often qualified but seldom succeeded in final-round play in the World Cup. Playing in 1930, 1950, 1954, 1958, 1962, 1966, 1970, 1978, and 1986, Mexico has a record of six wins, 17 defeats, and six draws, and has been outscored 64-27. If Mexico had not hosted the tournament in 1970 and 1986, the record would be much worse. Outside of Mexico, the record stands at one win, 16 defeats, and three ties while allowing 58 goals and scoring just 15. Mexico also holds the record for consecutive losses, with nine, from 1930 through 1958.

GIUSEPPE MEAZZA

THE PLAYER WHO scored a penalty
kick in a 1938 semifinal seconds before his
shorts fell to his ankles.

A master dribbler with a deadly accurate shot either on
the run or with a flick and pivot, Giuseppe Meazza led
Italy to World Cup titles in both 1934 and 1938. In the
1934 quarterfinals, Meazza scored the only goal on a
header to beat Spain 1-0. In the 1938 semifinals,
Meazza scored on a penalty kick seconds before his
ripped shorts fell to his ankles in a 2-1 triumph
over Brazil.

ROMANIA

THE ONLY NATION with a 40-year gap
between final-round victories.

Entering the 1994 tournament, Romania holds the
record for the longest span between victories. The
Romanians defeated Peru 3-1 in their first game of the
first World Cup tournament on July 14, 1930, in
Montevideo, Uruguay. Romania did not win another
final-round game until June 6, 1970, when it beat
Czechoslovakia 2-1 in Guadalajara, Mexico.

PEDRO CEA

THE FIRST PLAYER to score in an Olympic final and a World Cup final.

Pedro Cea of Uruguay became the first player to score in an Olympic final and a World Cup final in 1924 and 1930, respectively. In the Olympic gold medal match, Cea connected in a 3-0 win over Switzerland. He also had a goal in the first World Cup final, as Uruguay defeated Argentina 4-2.

JULIO CARDENOSA

THE PLAYER FROM Spain who became
famous for a goal he missed against Brazil.

In a game against Brazil on June 7, 1978, in Mar
del Plata, Argentina, Julio Cardenosa of Spain found
himself with the ball in front of an empty net with the
Brazilian defense in disarray. But Cardenosa hesitated too
long and failed to score. The game ended in a 0-0 draw.
Cardenosa made up for his horrendous mistake in Spain's
next match, four days later against Sweden in Buenos
Aires. He played brilliantly in Spain's 1-0 triumph.

TRINIDAD & TOBAGO

THE TEAM THAT the U.S. beat to
reach the finals for the first time since 1950.

When the U.S. met Trinidad & Tobago on
November 18, 1989, in Port of Spain, Trinidad, in the
deciding qualifying-round match for the 1990 World
Cup finals, both were hoping to change history. The U.S.
was attempting to reach the final round for the first time
in 40 years, and Trinidad & Tobago was trying for its
first final round ever. The U.S. had to win, while
Trinidad & Tobago only had to tie to qualify. The
U.S. pulled off the victory 1-0 on a Paul
Caligiuri goal volleyed in from about 25
yards in the 31st minute.

STOCKHOLM, SWEDEN

THE SMALLEST CROWD to witness a
World Cup final.

The World Cup final on June 29, 1958, between
Brazil and Sweden in Råsunda Stadium in Stockholm
was witnessed by a crowd of 49,737, the smallest ever
for a World Cup final. Brazil won 5-2.

MEXICO VS.
WEST GERMANY, 1986

THE FIRST 0-0 match in World Cup
history to be settled on penalty kicks.

In a quarterfinal match on June 21, 1986, in
Monterrey, Mexico, West Germany and Mexico battled
through a scoreless 120 minutes, causing the match to
be settled on penalty kicks. West Germany converted
four to one for Mexico to advance to the semifinals. The
one goal by Mexico is also the fewest any team has
scored in any of the eight World Cup matches through
1990 in which the winner has been determined on
penalty kicks.

BOBBY MOORE

THE ENGLISH STAR who was accused
of stealing just prior to the 1970 World Cup.

Bobby Moore, who was voted the outstanding
player of the 1966 World Cup, was a member of the
English team again four years later. On a tour of
Colombia prior to the 1970 tournament in Mexico,
Moore was accused of stealing a bracelet from a jewelry
store in Bogotá where the English team was staying.
Moore was detained for four days before being released
in time to play in the World Cup. Moore was ac-
quitted of all charges when it was revealed he
had been framed.

SOUTH KOREA

THE ONLY TEAM to allow 16 goals in consecutive matches.

South Korea was clearly overmatched in its first World Cup final-round appearance. The team lost 9-0 to Hungary on June 17, 1954, in Zurich, Switzerland, then three days later in Geneva, was routed 7-0 by Turkey. South Korea also qualified for the final round in 1986 and 1990, but is still looking for its first victory. It has seven losses and a draw in eight matches while being outscored 29-5.

UNITED STATES

THE NATION THAT shocked England with a victory in 1950.

In what many experts consider the most shocking upset not just in World Cup play but in the history of international soccer, the U.S. stunned England 1-0 on June 29, 1950, in Belo Horizonte, Brazil. The only goal was scored on a header by Haitian-born Joe Gaetjens, who was working as a dishwasher in a New York restaurant when he tried out for the World Cup squad. Gaetjens later played professionally in France, then returned to Haiti. The U.S. has not won a final-round game since its upset of England.

ALMEIDA REGO

THE REFEREE WHO mistakenly blew
time with six minutes left.

Almeida Rego of Brazil refereed the Argentina-
France match in Montevideo, Uruguay, on July 15,
1930. Argentina held a 1-0 lead with six minutes left
in the game when Marcel Langiller of France raced the
length of the field with the ball. As he closed in on the
goal, Rego blew his whistle to signal time had expired.
Argentina raced onto the field to celebrate and the
French followed in protest. It took mounted police
to clear the field so the game could continue. . .
France failed to score, and Argentina had a
controversial 1-0 victory.

SEPP MAIER

THE GOALKEEPER WHO has played in
the most World Cup final games.

Sepp Maier of West Germany holds the all-time
record for most games played in goal with 18 in 1970,
1974, and 1978. With Maier, West Germany won 11,
lost only three, and tied four, and won a championship
in 1974.

AUSTRIA VS. FRANCE, 1934

THE FIRST EXTRA-TIME match in World Cup play.

Austria and France were tied 1-1 at the end of 90 minutes on May 27, 1934, in Turin, Italy, forcing extra time. Austria went on to win 3-2.

NORTHERN IRELAND

THE TEAM THAT was under pressure not to play on Sundays.

Northern Ireland reached the World Cup final round for the first time in 1958 in Sweden, but was under pressure from the Ulster government not to play the two Sunday matches on its schedule. The team played anyway, and surprisingly reached the quarterfinals before losing 4-0 to France. The 1958 Northern Ireland team was the only one to prevent Italy from qualifying for the final round, by finishing ahead of the Italians five points to four. The climax was a 2-1 win over Italy on January 15 in Belfast.

ZAIRE

THE FIRST TEAM from central or southern Africa to qualify for the final round.

Zaire became both the first black-majority nation and the first African country from south of the Sahara Desert to qualify for the final round in 1974. Zaire's President Mobutu Sese Seko promised each player on the squad a house, a car, and a free vacation as a reward, then sent the team off to West Germany with the admonition "Win or die." Zaire was hopelessly outmatched, however, losing 2-0 to Scotland, 9-0 to Yugoslavia, and 3-0 to Brazil. Once the players returned home, their lives were spared, but the offer of free gifts was withdrawn.

74

MARACANA STADIUM

THE VENUE THAT held the largest crowd ever assembled for a World Cup final.

Maracana Stadium in Rio de Janeiro, Brazil, was the site of the 1950 World Cup final between Brazil and Uruguay, witnessed by a record crowd of 199,854. The largest stadium in the world, Maracana has a capacity of 220,000 with 178,000 seated and 42,000 standing. It was brand new, in fact not quite completed, when the World Cup opened.

75

TURKEY AND FRANCE

THE TWO NATIONS to withdraw from the final round in 1950 when they learned their travel itinerary.

Turkey and France were invited to participate in the final round of the World Cup in 1950 in Brazil, but declined when they learned they would have to play consecutive group matches as far as 2,000 miles apart.

PRINCE FAHID
OF KUWAIT

THE ONLY MEMBER of royalty to con-
vince a referee to disallow an opponent's goal.

France was leading Kuwait 3-1 in the 80th minute
on June 21, 1982, in Valladolid, Spain, when France's
Alain Giresse accepted a pass from Michel Platini and
volleyed in his team's fourth goal. The Kuwaiti players
argued with the referee that a spectator with a whistle
caused them to stop, believing that Giresse was offside.
During the Kuwaiti protest, Prince Fahid, who was
the president of the Kuwait FA, went onto the field
to appeal to the referee, Miroslav Stupar of the
USSR. The goal was disallowed, and
France scored again to win 4-1.

LEÓNIDAS

THE FIRST PLAYER to score four goals
in a World Cup final-round game.

At the 1938 World Cup in France, Brazil's
Leónidas (Leónidas da Silva) dazzled fans with a tour-
nament-high eight goals. In the first game of the draw,
against Poland on June 5 in Strasbourg, Leónidas
became the first player ever to score four goals in a final-
round game, although he accomplished the feat only
five minutes ahead of Ernst Willimowski, who scored
four for Poland in the same game. Brazil won 6-5.
Leónidas is best known as the perfecter of the
bicycle kick.

THE NETHERLANDS

THE ONLY NATION to lose back-to-back finals without ever claiming a championship.

The rise of Dutch soccer in the 1970s was a superb success story. The Netherlands reached the final round of the World Cup in 1974 for the first time since 1938. A 4-0 win over Argentina in the first game of the tournament was the first victory for the Netherlands in final-round competition. The Dutch reached the final but lost to West Germany 2-1. In 1978, the Netherlands again made it to the final, yet was defeated by Argentina 3-1.

NORMAN WHITESIDE

THE YOUNGEST PLAYER to appear in
a World Cup match.

Norman Whiteside of Northern Ireland became
the youngest player ever to appear in a final-round
game when he took the field at the age of 17 years, 42
days, breaking Pelé's record, on June 17, 1982, in a 0-0
tie with Yugoslavia at Zaragoza, Spain. Whiteside
played in each of the five matches Northern Ireland
played in the tournament. He was also in the final
round in 1986.

JAIRZINHO

THE PLAYER WHO scored a goal in every match for champion Brazil at the 1970 World Cup.

Jairzinho's (Jair Ventura Filho) cannonlike kicks produced goals in all six of Brazil's matches at the 1970 World Cup in Mexico. He had a total of seven as Brazil won all six matches. Jairzinho scored two in the first game, a 4-1 win over Czechoslovakia, the only goal in a 1-0 win over England, and one each in victories over Romania 3-2, Peru 4-2, Uruguay 3-1, and Italy 4-1 in the final.

WEST GERMANY
VS. AUSTRIA

THE 1982 MATCH that brought angry allegations of a fix.

West Germany and Austria met on June 25, 1982, in Gijón, Spain. West Germany needed to win to advance to the second round, while Austria could advance if it lost by fewer than three goals. If either team failed, Algeria would advance. West Germany scored in the 11th minute, and since the 1-0 score guaranteed both teams' entry to the second round, they proceeded to maneuver the ball without attempting to score. Algerian fans in the stands cried fix and jeered the teams. Neither West Germany nor Austria was later penalized.

INDIA

THE ONLY TEAM to withdraw from
the World Cup because the FIFA would not
let the members play barefoot.

India, which had gained independence from Great
Britain in 1947, looked forward to sending its own
team into World Cup play in 1950 in Brazil. India with-
drew, however, when the FIFA informed the players that
they could not play barefoot, as they had wished. India
has yet to qualify for the World Cup final round.

ITALY

THE ONLY NATION to win two World
Cups and an Olympic gold medal in soccer in
a four-year span.

Italy won World Cup titles in 1934 and 1938, and
won the gold medal in the 1936 Olympics in Berlin, all
within a four-year span. Italy is third behind only Brazil
and West Germany in the all-time World Cup standings
with 31 victories, 11 defeats, and 12 ties. The Italians
were the runner-up in 1970, finished fourth in 1978,
and hosted in 1934 and 1990. Italy has played in
the final round in 12 of the 14 World Cups,
missing only in 1930 and 1958.

URUGUAY

THE NATION TO go the most consecutive matches without scoring more than one
goal.

In recent years, Uruguay has become known for playing defense-minded matches. In a streak still alive as
the 1994 qualifying round commenced, Uruguay had
not scored multiple goals in 16 consecutive final-round
games, double the streak of any other nation. During
those 16 matches, Uruguay had two wins, nine defeats, and five draws, and had been outscored 24-7.

ALEX THÉPOT

THE GOALKEEPER WHO failed to last
more than 10 minutes in the first World Cup
match.

In the first World Cup game in history, on July 13,
1930, French goalkeeper Alex Thépot was kicked in the
jaw and suffered a concussion, necessitating his removal
from the game. Since no substitutions were allowed at
the time, France had to make do with 10 players and a
halfback in goal for the remainder of the contest.
France still won 4-1. Thépot returned for France's
two remaining games in the tournament, but
the French lost both, to Argentina 1-0 on
July 15 and 1-0 to Chile on July 19.

UWE SEELER AND
WLADISLAW ZMUDA

THE ONLY TWO players to make 21
appearances in final-round World Cup
matches.

Uwe Seeler of West Germany and Wladislaw Zmuda
of Poland share the record for most final-round games
played with 21. Seeler, perhaps the most popular player
in German soccer history, played for West Germany in
1958, 1962, 1966, and 1970, the latter two years as
captain. Zmuda was a member of Poland's World Cup
contingent in 1974, 1978, 1982, and 1986.

BRAZIL

THE ONLY NATION to win more than
40 World Cup games.

Brazil is the only nation to qualify for all 14 World
Cup final rounds and is the only nation to win more
than 40 final-round games. The country has won 44
games, lost 11, and tied 11, with three championships
(1958, 1962, and 1970). It has also been runner-up
once, and placed third twice, fourth once.

AUSTRIA VS.
SWITZERLAND, 1954

THE WORLD CUP game with the most
goals.

Austria and Switzerland participated in the highest-scoring game in World Cup history on June 26,
1954, in Lausanne, Switzerland, in a quarterfinal contest. The Swiss, roared on by the crowd, scored three in
the first 23 minutes. Austria then stunned Switzerland
by booting five into the net in the next 10 minutes. In
all, there were nine goals scored in a 23-minute stretch
of the first half. Austria led 5-4 at halftime, despite
missing a penalty, and won 7-5.

REPUBLIC OF IRELAND

THE NATION WITH the World Cup record for the lowest allowed-for goals per game.

The Republic of Ireland holds the record for the lowest goals against average, all-time, in World Cup play at 0.60 per match. The Irish qualified only once, in 1990, and played draws in their first four matches to set another record for most consecutive matches resulting in draws. They came against England (1-1), Egypt (0-0), the Netherlands (1-1), and Romania (0-0). The match against Romania was settled by penalties, with Ireland advancing 5-4. The Irish bowed out of the tournament with a 1-0 loss to Italy.

MEXICO AND ITALY

THE TWO NATIONS that have hosted
two World Cups.

Twelve different nations have hosted the 14 World
Cups, with Mexico and Italy each serving as host twice.
Mexico hosted in 1970 and 1986, while Italy was the
venue in 1934 and 1990. The others were Uruguay in
1930, France in 1938, Brazil in 1950, Switzerland in
1954, Sweden in 1958, Chile in 1962, England in
1966, West Germany in 1974, Argentina in 1978,
and Spain in 1982. The U.S. will host in 1994.

RENÉ VAN DE KERKHOF

THE PLAYER WHOSE cast caused a
controversy at the 1978 World Cup final.

René van de Kerkhof of the Netherlands injured
his arm in the first game of the 1978 tournament and
played in five subsequent games with a plastic cast pro-
tecting the injury without incident. But in the final
against Argentina, the Argentine captain, Daniel
Passarella, complained to referee Sergio Gonella of Italy
about the cast because he was concerned van de
Kerkhof would use it as a weapon. The referee
agreed, and the final was delayed for nine
minutes while the cast was replaced with
a soft bandage. Argentina went on
to win 3-1.

ADEMIR

THE ONLY BRAZILIAN to score nine
goals in a single World Cup tournament.

Ademir (Ademir Marques de Meneses) scored nine
goals for Brazil in the 1950 World Cup. An extraordi-
narily versatile player, Ademir began the 1950 tournament with two goals in a 4-0 win over Mexico, added
another in a 2-0 triumph over Yugoslavia, then exploded
for four scores in a 7-1 thrashing of Sweden. Ademir
scored two in Brazil's 6-1 win over Spain to reach the
final, but in the championship match, he was held
scoreless by Uruguay as Brazil succumbed in a
2-1 loss.

EL SALVADOR
AND HONDURAS

THE TWO NATIONS that participated
in the infamous "Soccer War."

Honduras and El Salvador met in a three-game
qualifying series in 1969 to advance to the final round
of the 1970 World Cup. Riots during the first two
games, fueled by long-smoldering animosities, burst
into an undeclared war on June 24, 1969, along the border between the two countries. Honduras had won the
first game 1-0 at home on June 8 and lost the second
3-0 in El Salvador on June 15. The third game,
played at a neutral site in Mexico City on June
28, resulted in a 3-2 El Salvador win.

ERIC WYNALDA

THE ONLY PLAYER from the U.S. to be
ejected from a final-round World Cup match.

Eric Wynalda became the first player from the U.S.
to be ejected from the final-round match on June 10,
1990, when he was red-carded by Swiss referee Kurt
Rothlisberger for a rough tackle against Czechoslovakia's
Josef Chovanec. After the World Cup, Wynalda became
the first U.S. player to play First Division soccer in
Germany.

ROMANIA AND PERU

THE TWO TEAMS that drew the smallest recorded crowd in the final round of a
World Cup tournament.

Romania and Peru had the misfortune of making their
World Cup debuts on July 14, 1930, in Montevideo,
which was Bastille Day, a public holiday in Uruguay.
The people in the Uruguayan capital were too busy cel-
ebrating to take much interest in the Romanian-
Peruvian match, and die-hard soccer fans were more
interested in the game between Brazil and
Yugoslavia across town. Before a crowd of only
300, Romania defeated Peru 3-1.

ZICO

THE PLAYER WHOSE goal was disallowed in 1978 because the referee blew time just before the ball hit the net.

With the score tied 1-1 between Brazil and Sweden on June 3, 1978, at Mar del Plata, Argentina, Zico of Brazil headed in a corner, but referee Clive Thomas of Wales blew his whistle for time a split second before the ball crossed the goal line. Brazil protested vehemently, but the score remained 1-1. Zico finally scored a goal that counted in a 3-0 win against Peru on June 14.

JUSTE FONTAINE

THE PLAYER WHO scored the most goals in a single World Cup.

Juste Fontaine was expected to be just a reserve for France in the 1958 World Cup tournament in Sweden, but finished with an all-time-record 13 goals. Born in Marrakesh, Morocco, Fontaine moved to France when he turned professional. In the third-place match of the 1958 Cup, he tied a World Cup record with four goals in a 6-3 win over West Germany. He also scored three times against Paraguay in the first game of the tournament, a 7-3 win.

FINLAND

THE ONLY TEAM to lose a qualifying-round match at home by 10 goals.

Finland played the mighty USSR on July 27, 1957, in Moscow and lost only 2-1, so the team felt confident going into the return match on August 15 in Helsinki. Finland lost 10-0 to the Soviets, however, the worst defeat by a team on its own soil. Finland has never qualified for the final round in a World Cup.

ENGLAND

THE TEAM THAT won its only World Cup title in 1966.

England shook off years of disappointment in World Cup play to win in 1966. England had never reached the World Cup semifinals, though team manager Alf Ramsey guided such stars as Bobby Moore, Bobby Charlton, Gordon Banks, Nobby Stiles, Geoff Hurst, and Roger Hunt to victory. Playing at home, at Wembley Stadium in London, was also an advantage. In the quarterfinals, England took care of Argentina 1-0 and reached the final with a 2-1 triumph over Portugal. In the final, England downed West Germany 4-2 in extra time.

NIGERIA

THE COUNTRY DISQUALIFIED from the World Cup in 1973 because of its participation in a riot.

Nigeria and Ghana squared off on February 10, 1973, in the qualifying rounds for the 1974 World Cup in Lagos, Nigeria, in a match that ended in a riot. In the closing stages, Ghana scored a goal that put it ahead 3-2, but the crowd thought Ghana should have been called for offsides. Spectators started fires in the stands and hurled bottles, cans, and rocks onto the field. Officials called off the match, and troops were brought in to restore order. Nigeria was disqualified by the FIFA, and Ghana advanced to the next round.

101

JUAN SCHIAFFINO

THE PLAYER WHO scored five goals for
Uruguay in the 1950 World Cup and later
played on the Italian team.

Juan Schiaffino scored five goals for Uruguay in 1950
in leading his nation to a World Cup title. Playing inside left, Schiaffino scored four goals in an 8-0 win over
Bolivia in Uruguay's opener and one in the final, a 2-1
triumph over host Brazil. Schiaffino also played for
Uruguay in the 1954 World Cup, then moved to Italy
to play professionally. He was a member of the
1958 Italian national team, but despite his
presence, Italy failed to survive the qualifying round for the only time in its
history.

102

FRANZ BECKENBAUER

THE ONLY INDIVIDUAL to serve as captain of one West German champion and manager of another.

Franz Beckenbauer was the captain of West Germany's 1974 World Cup champions and the team manager in 1990. He also played for the West German team that lost in the final to England in 1966 and for the team that finished third in 1970. The most complete player ever to hail from Germany, Beckenbauer was named manager of the national team in 1984. His compatriots reached the final in 1986 before winning the 1990 title.

103

BRAZIL VS. SWEDEN, 1958

THE WORLD CUP final with the most goals.

Brazil won its first championship against host Sweden on June 29, 1958, in the highest-scoring final in Cup history. Sweden drew first on a goal by Nils Liedholm, but Brazil soared ahead with two goals by Vavá for a 2-1 halftime lead. Pelé scored for Brazil in the 55th minute and was followed by Mario Zagalo's goal in the 68th minute for a 4-1 lead. Agne Simonsson scored for Sweden in the 80th minute, but it was too late. Pelé's second goal in the final seconds of play gave Brazil a 5-2 win.

PORTUGAL

THE ONLY TEAM to beat West Germany in a qualifying-round match.

West Germany has an incredible record of 35 wins, eight draws, and only one defeat in World Cup qualifying competition. The only defeat came at the hands of Portugal by a 1-0 score on October 16, 1985, in Stuttgart, West Germany. The win helped Portugal qualify for the final round for the first time since 1966.

EL SALVADOR

THE ONLY NATION to play more than three final-round games without earning a victory or a draw.

El Salvador has lost all six of the World Cup final-round matches in which it has participated and has been outscored 22-1. In 1970 in Mexico, El Salvador lost 3-0 to Belgium, 4-0 to Mexico, and 2-0 to the USSR. In 1982 in Spain, El Salvadoreans fell 10-1 to Hungary, 1-0 to Belgium, and 2-0 to Argentina. It is somehow fitting that in the only game in which El Salvador scored a goal, it surrendered the most goals in World Cup final-round history.

PAOLO ROSSI

THE PLAYER WHO put his team into
the semifinals in 1982 with three tie-break-
ing goals in one game.

In 24 final-round games and 16 qualifying-round
matches since 1966, no team had ever scored three goals
in a game against a Brazilian World Cup squad. In an
upset on July 5, 1982, Paolo Rossi of Italy scored three
all by himself to put Italy in the semifinals by a score of
3-2. The performance was a complete surprise, because
Rossi had been held scoreless through the first four
games of the tournament. He led the tournament with six goals and is the only top
scorer held scoreless in as many initial games.

DOGAN BABACAN

THE INDIVIDUAL WHOSE house was
robbed while refereeing a World Cup match.

Dogan Babacan of Turkey was the referee for the
opening match of the 1974 World Cup, played between West Germany and Chile on June 14 in West
Berlin. Babacan's wife and daughter in Istanbul went to
a neighbor's house to watch the game on television, and
while there, the Babacan family home was burglarized.

SPAIN, THE NETHERLANDS, ITALY, SWEDEN, AND HUNGARY

THE FIVE NATIONS that boycotted the first World Cup because they were passed over as hosts.

Spain, the Netherlands, Italy, Sweden, and Hungary were among the contenders to host the first World Cup in 1930. The FIFA chose Uruguay as the site of the tournament, and the four losers angrily agreed to boycott the tournament, which remained a sore point in European–Latin American soccer relations for decades.

MUAMBA KAZADI

THE ONLY GOALKEEPER to be removed from a World Cup match for reasons
other than injury.

Muamba Kazadi of Zaire became the only goalkeeper
in World Cup history to be removed for reasons other
than injury, on June 18, 1974, against Yugoslavia in
Gelsenkirchen, West Germany. Kazadi was removed
after 18 minutes and Zaire trailing 3-0 by coach
Blagoje Vidinić and replaced by Dimbi Tubilandu.
The move made a bad situation worse. Yugoslavia
scored three more goals in Tubilandu's first 16
minutes in goal, and went on to win 9-0.

ENGLAND

THE DEFENDING TEAM that had trouble sleeping because of noisy hosts.

England won the World Cup in 1966, but had few friends in Latin America. The rivalry intensified at the 1970 World Cup in Mexico. The English brought their own bottled water and sausage and bacon, but by Mexican law, the food supplies were destroyed upon arrival. Before their second match against Brazil, the English players were "serenaded" at 3 a.m. by a couple hundred Mexicans, most of them equipped with drums, frying pans, horns, and other noisemakers. Somehow, the sleepless players reached the quarterfinals of the tournament.

111

CZECHOSLOVAKIA

THE ONLY TEAM to win a match settled in extra time by three goals.

Czechoslovakia and the Netherlands battled through 90 minutes of scoreless soccer on June 5, 1938, in Le Havre, France, to force extra time. In the additional 30 minutes, the Czechs wasted no time putting the Dutch away with three goals for a 3-0 win.

TUNISIA

THE FIRST TEAM from Africa to win a final-round game.

When Tunisia took the field against Mexico on June 2, 1978, in Rosario, Argentina, African nations had not fared well in the final round. The three previous teams to go that far were Egypt in 1934, Morocco in 1970, and Zaire in 1974, and they combined to lose five and tie one while being outscored 24-4. Tunisia beat Mexico 3-1, however, then lost only 1-0 to Poland and held West Germany to a scoreless tie.

113

PELÉ

THE ONLY PLAYER to play on three
World Cup champions.

The most celebrated player of all time, Pelé (Edson
Arantes do Nascimento) is the only individual to play
on three World Cup champions. He did so while a
member of Brazil's national team in 1958, 1962, and
1970. Pelé gained international recognition at the 1958
World Cup in Sweden as a 17-year-old with six goals,
despite missing the first two matches with an injury.
Injuries also reduced his playing time in 1962 and
1966, but in 1970 he had his first injury-free
World Cup and scored four goals.

URUGUAY

THE ONLY NATION to fail to defend its World Cup title.

For a variety of reasons Uruguay chose not to compete in the World Cup in Italy in 1934 after winning the championship in 1930. The Uruguayans were still miffed that only four European nations (France, Yugoslavia, Romania, and Belgium) traveled to Uruguay for the 1930 games, the 1934 team was a shadow of the 1930 winners, and the nation was faced with a players' strike. In addition, European clubs were raiding South American clubs for top talent.

115

JIMMY DICKINSON

THE PLAYER WHO cost England a
victory in 1954 by heading the ball into his
own net.

England held a 3-1 lead over Belgium with 15 minutes
left in the match on June 17, 1954, in Basel,
Switzerland, but Belgium came back to tie 3-3 and force
extra time. England led 4-3 in the extra 30 minutes, but
a long Belgian free kick struck the head of England's
Jimmy Dickinson and bounced into the English net to
tie the score at 4-4, where it remained when time
expired.

BELGIUM, BRAZIL, FRANCE, ROMANIA, AND YUGOSLAVIA

THE FIVE NATIONAL teams to arrive on the same boat at the first World Cup.

Belgium, France, Romania, and Yugoslavia were the only four European nations to participate in the first World Cup in Uruguay in 1930. All four teams traveled from Europe on the same boat on a trip that took a bone-wearying three weeks. The boat stopped along the way to pick up the team from Brazil, and was greeted in Uruguay with great fanfare.

CZECHOSLOVAKIA

THE ONLY NATION to lose two World Cup finals after scoring the first goal of the match.

The team that has scored the first goal of a World Cup final has been somewhat jinxed throughout the years. In the 14 World Cup finals, the team that scored first lost seven times, including five in a row between 1950 and 1966. Czechoslovakia is the only nation to score first in two losing finals, first in 1934 in a 2-1 loss to Italy and again in 1962 in a 3-1 defeat at the hands of Brazil.

Czechoslovakia has qualified for the final round eight times, and has a record of 11 wins, 14 losses, and five draws.

WALTER ZENGA

THE ONLY GOALKEEPER to be unbeaten in 517 consecutive minutes in World
Cup play.

Playing for Italy in 1990, Walter Zenga was unscored
upon during the first five games of the tournament. He
was not beaten until the 67th minute of the semifinal on
July 3 against Argentina in Naples, Italy, a game that
ended in a 1-1 tie after extra time before Argentina won
on penalties 4-3. Zenga beat the old record of 499
minutes, set by Peter Shilton of England in 1982
and 1986. Zenga and Shilton squared off in
goal in the third-place playoff in 1990 on
July 7 in Bari, Italy. The Italians
won 2-1.

119

WEST GERMANY VS.
EAST GERMANY, 1974

THE ONLY WORLD Cup final-round
match between the two Germanys.

East Germany reached the World Cup final round
only once, and it seemed fitting that the East Germans
would meet the West Germans in one of the matches.
It happened in the third game of first-round group play
on June 22, 1974, in Hamburg. Security was tight, but
the only shocking action was on the field. East Germany
won 1-0 on a goal by Jürgen Sparwasser with 10 minutes left. After the match, West Germany won four
in a row to win the championship. The East
Germans lost two and tied one.

ANDRES MAZZALI

THE URUGUAYAN GOALKEEPER who
was kicked off the 1930 team for sneaking
out of the team hotel.

Andres Mazzali starred for the Uruguayan team in goal
at the 1924 and 1928 Olympics. He led his nation to
two gold medals, allowing just seven goals in 10 games.
He was expected to do the same at the World Cup in
1930, but was kicked off the team for breaking training. The Uruguayans trained for two months in a lux-
ury hotel in Prado Park in Montevideo. One night,
the lonely Mazzali left to visit his family. He
was replaced by Enrique Ballesteros.
Uruguay went on to capture the first
World Cup.

121

NORWAY

THE NATION THAT lost to the defending and eventual champion in extra time in
the only final-round game in its history.

Norway has played only one game in the final round in
World Cup play, but it was a historically significant
one. Norway played Italy on June 5, 1938, in Marseilles,
France, and was a huge underdog against the Italian jug-
gernaut, which had won the World Cup in 1934. Italy
scored in the first two minutes of play, but Norway
evened the score 1-1 in the second half to force
extra time. Italy barely escaped with a 2-1 win,
and went on to win the World Cup again.

CHILE

THE SOUTH AMERICAN nation that finished third as World Cup host.

Chile has participated in the final round of the World Cup in 1930, 1950, 1962, 1966, 1974, and 1982, with a record of seven wins, 11 defeats, and three ties. Chile's greatest moment was a third-place finish as the host nation in 1962. In the third-place playoff, Chile defeated Yugoslavia 1-0 on a goal by Eladio Rojas, his second of the tournament.

ROMANIA

THE TEAM HAND-PICKED by the nation's reigning monarch.

Romania sent a team to the first World Cup in 1930 in Uruguay only at the intervention of their reigning monarch, King Carol, who chose the players himself and lobbied with their employers to give them three months off to participate in the tournament. Romania beat Peru 3-1, but lost 4-0 to Uruguay.

GEOFF HURST

THE ONLY PLAYER to score three goals in a World Cup final.

With West Germany shadowing England's Bobby Charlton all over the field in the 1966 World Cup final, played on July 30 at Wembley Stadium in London, Geoff Hurst broke free for a World Cup final record of three goals. Hurst scored two of his goals, one of them a header, in extra time as England defeated West Germany 4-2 for the championship. Hurst is also the only player to score a header in a World Cup final.

PEDRO MONZON

THE FIRST PLAYER to be ejected from a World Cup final.

Pedro Monzon of Argentina was the first player ever to be ejected from a World Cup final on July 8, 1990, in a 1-0 loss to West Germany. A 46th-minute substitute, Monzon was sent off 18 minutes later for clobbering West Germany's Jürgen Klinsmann. Monzon was joined on the sidelines in the 87th minute by team-mate Gustavo Dezotti, who was also ejected for rough play. Argentina had to finish the game with nine players.

ITALY

THE WINNER OF the last World Cup
before the outbreak of World War II.

Italy was attempting to win its second consecutive
title when it took the field against Hungary in Paris,
France, on June 19, 1938. Italy struck first on a goal by
Gino Colaussi in the fifth minute. Hungary evened matters at 1-1 in the seventh minute, but Italy scored twice
before intermission on goals by Silvio Piola in the 16th
minute and by Colaussi in the 35th minute. György
Sárosi of Hungary pulled his team to within one
goal with a score in the 70th minute, but Piola
scored again in the 82nd minute to make
the final score 4-2 Italy.

127

SCOTLAND

THE TEAM THAT refused to play in the
final round of the 1950 World Cup because it
did not finish first in its qualifying group.

The FIFA decreed that for the 1950 World Cup the top
two finishers from a group consisting of British Isles
teams from England, Scotland, Northern Ireland, and
Wales would qualify for the final round. Scotland refused
to go unless it finished first, however, and came in second in the group after a 1-0 defeat to England. No
amount of persuading could change the minds of
the Scottish, and they stayed home rather than
travel to Brazil for the final round.

PERU

THE TEAM THAT Argentina beat amid controversy to reach the 1978 World Cup final.

Argentina took the field against Peru on June 21, 1978, in Rosario, Argentina, needing not just to win to reach the World Cup final, but to win by scoring at least four goals and winning by at least three. If Argentina failed, Brazil would advance to play the Netherlands for the championship. Argentina won 6-0, causing Brazilians to level allegations of a fix. Peru's goal-keeper was Ramón Quiroga, who was born in Argentina but acquired Peruvian citizen-ship and became eligible for that country's national team.

ALDO DONELLI

THE PLAYER WHO scored the only
goal for the U.S. in the 1934 World Cup.

Aldo "Buff" Donelli scored the only U.S. goal in
the 1934 World Cup in a 7-1 loss to host Italy.
Donelli, who was born in Naples, Italy, and moved to
the U.S. as a child, stayed behind after the Cup to play
soccer professionally in Italy. When he returned to the
U.S., Donelli became the only individual to coach pro
and college football teams simultaneously. He was
coach of Duquense University in 1941 and for part
of the season was head coach of the Pittsburgh
Steelers.

WEST GERMANY
VS. POLAND, 1974

THE SEMIFINAL THAT was delayed to
remove water from the field.

When West Germany met Poland on July 3, 1974,
in Frankfurt to decide who would advance to the final, a
downpour struck an hour before the match, causing a 30-
minute delay while the fire department pumped thousands of gallons of water from the field. Players had to
scoop the ball out of the water instead of making ground
passes. Poland had won all five of its previous matches
by an aggregate score of 15-4, but lost this one 1-0.
West Germany won on a goal by Gerd Müller,
who deflected a shot by Uli Hoeness 14
minutes from the end.

MEXICO

THE TEAM THAT traveled all the way
to Rome for the 1934 World Cup, only to
lose a qualifying match.

In a case of misguided logic, the FIFA had the United
States and Mexico play a qualifying match in Rome on
May 24, 1934, three days before the start of the final
round of the tournament. The U.S. won the game 4-2.
Mexico had traveled all the way to Italy for the World
Cup and did not even get the opportunity to play in
the final round. In the opening match, May 27, the
U.S. was defeated by Italy 7-1.

TAIWAN

THE ONLY TEAM to be outscored by
35 goals in the qualifying round.

Taiwan's entry in the 1986 qualifying round was
far from a success. It resulted in six defeats in six
matches by a combined score of 36-1. Taiwan lost 6-0
and 5-0 to Israel, 5-1 and 5-0 to New Zealand, and 7-0
and 8-0 to Australia.

BELGIUM

THE TEAM THAT stunned the defending champion in the opening game of the
1982 World Cup.

World Cup play in 1982 began on June 13 in
Barcelona, Spain, with defending champion Argentina
facing Belgium. In a stunning upset, Belgium won 1-0
on Erwin Vandenbergh's goal 17 minutes into the second half. It was Belgium's first win in the final round
since 1970. Previously, there had never been a goal
scored in the first game of a tournament since the
World Cup began the practice of starting play
with a single opening day match in 1966.

WALES

THE TEAM THAT qualified for the
1958 final round in a lottery.

Wales qualified for the final round of the World
Cup in 1958, for the only time in its history, in a
round-about way. Wales finished second in its qualifying group and was therefore eliminated. But the Welsh
team was chosen in a lottery among the 13 second-place
teams to face Israel in a three-game playoff, and Wales
won to earn a World Cup berth in Sweden. Once
there, Wales reached the quarterfinals with a win
and three draws before being knocked out of
the tournament by Brazil 1-0 on a goal by
Pelé.

VAVÁ

THE ONLY PLAYER to score goals in
successive World Cup finals.

Vavá led Brazil to back-to-back World Cup championships in 1958 and 1962 with some brilliant play
in the final. In 1958, he scored twice in Brazil's 5-2 win
over Sweden in Stockholm. In 1962, Vavá scored once as
Brazil took Czechoslovakia 3-1 in Santiago, Chile.

SALVATORE SCHILLACI

THE PLAYER WHO began the 1990 World Cup on the bench and finished as the tournament's leading scorer.

Salvatore Schillaci was the last player chosen for the 1990 Italian World Cup team, began the tournament on the bench, and finished as the leading scorer with six goals. Schillaci entered the first game against Austria in Rome as a 74th-minute substitute, but four minutes later scored the only goal of the match to give Italy a 1-0 win. Schillaci did not earn a start until Italy's third game, but he scored a goal in each of his country's final five matches, including the third-place playoff in which Italy defeated England 2-1.

137

URUGUAY

THE SMALLEST NATION to win a
World Cup.

Despite having a current population of just over 3
million, Uruguay has had an extraordinary impact on international soccer. It is, by far, the smallest nation to win
a World Cup. Uruguay hosted and won the first World
Cup tournament in 1930, and after withdrawing in 1934
and 1938, it won again in 1950. Uruguay also finished in
fourth place in 1954 and 1970 and had an overall record
of 15 wins, 14 losses, and eight ties. It also qualified
in 1962, 1966, 1974, 1986, and 1990. From
1974 through 1990, however, Uruguay's
final-round record is one victory, six
defeats, and four draws.

FRANTISEK PLÁNIČKA AND GIAMPIERO COMBI

THE ONLY TWO goalkeepers to face each other as captains in a World Cup final.

Frantisek Pláníčka of Czechoslovakia and Giampiero Combi of Italy faced each other both as opposite goalkeepers and as captains in the 1934 World Cup final. It is the only time that two goalkeepers served as captains in the same final. Italy won 2-1 in extra time. The two stifled the opposition for most of the match. It was 70 minutes before a goal was scored.

139

HUNGARY
VS. BRAZIL, 1954

THE WORLD CUP match that led to a
nasty fight inside the locker rooms.

Hungary and Brazil played a quarterfinal match in
a pelting rain on June 27, 1954, in Switzerland, which
has become known as the notorious "Battle of Berne."
Hungary went up 2-0 after eight minutes and held on to
win 4-2. The teams spent as much time kicking each
other as they did booting the ball. After the game, the
Brazilians hid in the tunnel leading to the locker
rooms and waited for the Hungarians. The teams
fought for 20 minutes and sustained several
casualties.

ALGERIA

THE TEAM THAT upset West Germany in 1982 in its first final-round game.

West Germany qualified for the 1982 World Cup final round by winning all eight games by a combined score of 33-3. In its first game in the finals, on June 16 in Gijón, Spain, West Germany faced Algeria, which qualified for the first time. Algeria engineered a huge upset by a 2-1 score. Rabah Madjer scored the first goal of the game in the 53rd minute, then set up Lakhdar Belloumi on the second, 16 minutes later, to break a 1-1 tie. Algeria also stunned Chile 3-2. West Germany recovered to reach the final before losing to Italy.

DIEGO MARADONA

THE PLAYER WHO scored the much-
disputed goal in the 1986 Argentina-
England match.

Argentina and England, bitter rivals, met in the quarterfinals on June 22, 1986, in Mexico City. Five minutes
into the second half, Diego Maradona scored the first goal
of the game. Television replays showed Maradona appar-
ently hit the ball with his hand, but Tunisian referee Ali
Bennaceur ruled that Maradona headed the ball into the
netting. Maradona scored again later in the game,
and this was typical of his brilliance, as he drib-
bled nearly half the length of the field
through four English defenders.
Argentina won 2-1.

142

JIMMY KEMP

THE SCOTTISH FAN who renounced
his heritage after the 1978 World Cup.

Jimmy Kemp, a Scottish hospital cook, was so dis-
gusted by Scotland's play in the World Cup in 1978
that he took space in a local newspaper to announce that
in the future he wished to be regarded as an Englishman
and would be taking elocution lessons to rid himself of
his Scottish accent.

ANATOLY PUSATCH

THE FIRST SUBSTITUTE to play in a World Cup match.

Substitutions were not permitted in World Cup play until 1970. The first was Anatoly Pusatch of the USSR, who was inserted into the game against Mexico on May 31, 1970, in Mexico City. The game ended in a scoreless tie. In the USSR's three subsequent matches, Pusatch was a starter in one and failed to appear in the other two.

144

FRANCE

THE ONLY NATION to play in the third-place game at least three times without ever reaching the final.

France has played for third place in the World Cup three times, with wins in 1958 and 1986 and a defeat in 1982, but has never played in the final. France has qualified for the final round in 1930, 1934, 1954, 1958, 1966, 1978, 1982, and 1986, and has an overall record of 15 wins, 14 losses, and five draws.

BOLIVIA

THE ONLY NATION to allow more
than 15 goals in final-round play without
scoring.

Bolivia has been outscored 16-0 in three defeats in
final-round play. In 1930 in Uruguay, the Bolivians lost
4-0 to Yugoslavia and 4-0 to Brazil. In 1950 in Brazil,
the team was hammered by Uruguay 8-0. Bolivia has
failed to qualify for the final round in the always tough
South American region since that 1950 debacle.

1954 AND 1990
WORLD CUPS

THE HIGHEST- AND lowest-scoring tournaments.

The 26 games of the 1954 World Cup produced 140 goals, or an average of 5.38 goals per game, the highest in history. The next tournament, in 1958, saw teams play 35 games and combine to score 126 goals, or 3.60 goals per game, which was then an all-time low. By 1962, defense-minded soccer had taken hold, and only 2.78 goals have been scored per contest. There has not been a single tournament in which teams averaged at least three goals a game since 1958. The low was in 1990, when only 115 goals were scored in 52 matches, an average of 2.21 per game.

WEST GERMANY
VS. ITALY, 1970

THE ONLY FINAL-ROUND game to produce five extra-time goals.

The semifinal match between West Germany and Italy on July 17, 1970, in Mexico City was tied 1-1 after 90 minutes of play. The 30 minutes of extra time saw the two teams combine for an unprecedented five goals, with Italy achieving victory 4-3. The winner was scored by substitute Gianni Rivera in the 112th minute.

148

ROGER MILLA

THE OLDEST PLAYER to score a goal in a World Cup.

Roger Milla of Cameroon became the oldest player to score a goal in World Cup final-round history in 1990 when he connected four times at the age of 38. Milla was coaxed out of semiretirement to play in the 1990 tournament. He came into Cameroon's second game as a 58th-minute substitute and scored two goals in the final 15 minutes to give Cameroon a 2-1 win over Romania. In the game against Colombia, Milla arrived in the 54th minute and scored twice in extra time as Cameroon won 2-1.

DORTMUND,
WEST GERMANY

THE ONLY WORLD Cup venue to over-
look a nudist colony.

The soccer stadium in Dortmund, West Germany,
used for World Cup games involving Sweden, the
Netherlands, Brazil, and Bulgaria in 1974, overlooked
a nudist camp, much to the distraction of both the
spectators and the members of the clothes-optional
community.

VITTORIO POZZO

THE ONLY INDIVIDUAL to manage two teams to a World Cup title.

Vittorio Pozzo of Italy is the only individual to manage two teams that went all the way to the World Cup championships. He accomplished the feat in 1934 and 1938.

ANTONIO RATTÍN

THE PLAYER WHO refused to leave the
field for eight minutes after being ejected
from a 1966 quarterfinal.

England and Argentina met on July 23, 1966, in
London in a bruising quarterfinal match that kept West
German referee Rudolf Kreitlein busy. Nine minutes
from halftime, he ejected Argentina's Antonio Rattín for
"violence of the tongue." Rattín refused to leave the
field for eight minutes. England scored in the second
half on a header by Geoff Hurst and held on to win
1-0. Afterward, Argentina's players began
pummeling Kreitlein, who was rescued by
police.

BRAZIL

THE ONLY HEAVILY favored team to lose a final at home.

When Uruguay met Brazil for the World Cup title on July 16, 1950, in Rio de Janeiro, they were 10-1 underdogs. Brazil was considered to be the vastly superior team and had the advantage of playing at home. The first half was scoreless, but just after intermission, Friaça of Brazil scored. Uruguay's Juan Schiaffino evened matters at 1-1 in the 66th minute. With 11 minutes to play, Uruguay went up 2-1 when Alcides Ghiggia drove in low inside the near post, and held on for the upset win.

153

SWEDEN

THE NATION THAT has hosted a
World Cup and played in a final, but has not
won a match since 1974.

Sweden has had some success in early World Cup tournaments, but little lately. Qualifying for the final round in 1934, 1938, 1950, 1958, 1970, 1974, 1978, and 1990, Sweden was runner-up as host in 1958, finished third in 1950, and fourth in 1938. The last Swedish victory in the final round was in 1974 when they defeated Yugoslavia 2-1. Overall, Sweden's World Cup record is 11 wins, 14 losses, and six draws.

DINO ZOFF

THE OLDEST INDIVIDUAL to play on a World Cup champion.

Born on February 28, 1942, Dino Zoff was 40 years old and in goal for each of Italy's seven matches during the 1982 World Cup in Spain. He allowed just six goals during the tournament as Italy won with a 3-1 final win over West Germany on July 11 in Madrid. Zoff also played goalkeeper for Italy in the World Cup in 1974 and 1978. Zoff was noted for his agility, courage, anticipation, and consistency. He was unbeaten in 12 consecutive international matches between 1972 and 1974 for a record of 1,143 minutes.

155

HUNGARY

THE FIRST TEAM to defeat Uruguay in World Cup play.

When Uruguay met Hungary in a semifinal match on June 30, 1954, in Lausanne, Switzerland, Uruguay had 10 wins and a draw in its 11 World Cup matches, while Hungary had been undefeated in international competition for four years. Hungary took a 2-0 lead in the game, but Uruguay roared back to force the game into extra time. In the extra 30 minutes, Sandor Kocsis of Hungary scored on headers for his 10th and 11th goals of the tournament, and Hungary held on to win 4-2.

WEST GERMANY
AND BRAZIL

THE ONLY TWO nations to play in over 55 World Cup matches.

West Germany has played in the most World Cup matches, with 68, while Brazil is second at 66. Brazil has won the most games with 44. West Germany's 39 is second. Brazil has qualified for all 14 final rounds, West Germany for all 12 it has entered. Each has three championships. The all-time dream World Cup matchup would seem to be West Germany versus Brazil, but it has never happened. Amazingly, the two powers have never met in the World Cup final round.

HAITI

THE TEAM THAT broke Italy's streak of
being unscored upon in 13 consecutive international matches.

Haitian President Jean-Claude Duvalier was so happy
about his team's achievement of reaching the final round
of the World Cup for the first time in 1974 that he offered
his players a $300,000 bonus for a win and a $200,000
bonus for a draw. In the first game, Haiti took a 1-0 lead
over Italy on a goal by Emmanuel Sanon early in the
second half, the first time the Italians had been
scored on in 13 consecutive international
matches dating back to September 1972.
Italy went on to win 3-1, and Haiti
lost its other two matches.

158

GUILLERMO STÀBILE

THE LEADING SCORER in the first World Cup.

Guillermo Stàbile of Argentina was the top scorer with eight goals in the 1930 World Cup. He did not play in the first game, a 1-0 win over France, but was inserted into the line-up in the second contest to replace a player who went back home to take a university exam. Well-rested, Stàbile scored three times in Argentina's 6-3 triumph over Mexico. He added two more to help beat Chile 3-1 and booted two home in the semifinals as Argentina won 6-1 over the U.S. Stàbile scored again in the final, but Argentina lost 4-2 to Uruguay.

MAURO BELLUGI

THE PLAYER WHO was pulled in the quickest substitution in World Cup history.

Mauro Bellugi of Italy was replaced by Antonello Cuccureddu after only six minutes of a match against Argentina on June 10, 1978, in Buenos Aires in the quickest substitution in World Cup history. Italy won the match 1-0.

WEST GERMANY

THE ONLY NATION to play in a World Cup final six times.

West Germany has played in six of the last 10 World Cup finals, with victories in 1954, 1974, and 1990. In the all-time World Cup standings, which include Germany's pre–World War II record, West Germany has 39 wins, 14 defeats, and 15 ties. It has qualified for the final round every year except 1930, when it did not enter, and 1950, when it was ineligible in the aftermath of the war. In 1994, Germany will again field one team in the World Cup as a result of the reunification of the East and West.

161

TRINIDAD

THE NATION THAT lost a place in the
1974 final round because it had four goals
disallowed in a qualifying match.

Trinidad had four goals disallowed by a Salvadoran referee in a qualifying match against Haiti on December
4, 1973, in Port-au-Prince, Haiti. Haiti won 2-1, which
allowed it to reach the final round for the only time in
its history. If just one of the four disallowed goals had
counted, Trinidad would have been in the final round
for the only time in its short history as a nation.

PEDRO DORADO

THE FIRST PLAYER to score a goal in a
World Cup final.

Pedro Dorado of Uruguay was the first player to
score in a World Cup final with a goal in the 12th
minute of Uruguay's 4-2 win over Argentina on July
30, 1930, in Montevideo. It was Dorado's second World
Cup goal. The first was against Romania in a 4-0 win on
July 22.

PONTIAC SILVERDOME

THE FIRST INDOOR field to be used in the final round.

The U.S. plays host to the first World Cup matches in North America in 1994. One of the 10 stadiums where matches are scheduled is the Pontiac Silverdome in Pontiac, Michigan, the first indoor facility to be used in a final round in World Cup history. The artificial turf field at the Silverdome will be replaced by grass. The first indoor facility used in the qualifying round was the Kingdome in Seattle, Washington, where the U.S. defeated Canada 2-0 on October 20, 1976.

BRAZIL VS. ITALY, 1970

THE WORLD CUP final played for permanent possession of the Jules Rimet Trophy.

The FIFA declared that the first nation to win three Cup titles would retain the Jules Rimet Trophy permanently, not just for four years. Brazil and Italy had both won twice when they met in the final on June 21, 1970, in Mexico City. Brazil scored first on a goal by Pelé in the 18th minute, but Italy equalized 19 minutes later. Brazil thrilled the fans with three goals in the second half, by Gérson, Jairzinho, and Carlos Alberto, for a 4-1 win. A new trophy, called the FIFA World Cup, was commissioned for the 1974 tournament.

MOROCCO

THE FIRST AFRICAN team to reach the
second round of the World Cup finals.

The 1986 team from Morocco became the first
from an African nation to survive the first round of the
World Cup. In the initial group phase, Morocco had
scoreless duels with Poland and England, then defeated
Portugal 3-1. In the second round, Morocco's dreams
were upended in a 1-0 loss to West Germany.

GARRINCHA

THE PLAYER WHO overcame polio to
star in the 1958 and 1962 finals.

Some call Garrincha (Manual Francisco dos Santos)
the greatest dribbler of all time. Nicknamed after a
Portuguese expression meaning "little bird," Garrincha
suffered as a child from polio, which made one of his legs
shorter than the other. As a result, his movements on the
field were unpredictable and very difficult to defend. He
scored two goals in the quarterfinals and two more in
the semifinals in 1962 World Cup action. Brazil
won in both 1958 and 1962.

COLOMBIA

THE COUNTRY THAT backed out of hosting the 1986 World Cup.

Colombia was originally slated to host the 1986 World Cup, but the South American nation had to give up the venture in 1983 because of economic difficulties. Brazil, Canada, Mexico, and the U.S. all vied to take Colombia's place. Mexico was the final choice.

BRAZIL

THE ONLY NATION to put together a
13-game unbeaten streak in World Cup play.

Brazil had a 13-game unbeaten streak from 1958
through 1966 in World Cup final-round play, which
included 11 wins and two draws, and championships in
1958 and 1962. The streak ended on July 15, 1966, in a
3-1 loss to Hungary in Liverpool, England. Ironically,
Brazil's previous defeat in World Cup play had also
come at the hands of Hungary in the infamous Battle
of Berne in 1954.

DIRK NANNINGA

THE FIRST SUBSTITUTE to score in a World Cup final.

Dirk Nanninga of the Netherlands became the first substitute to score in a World Cup final on June 25, 1978, against Argentina in Buenos Aires. Nanninga scored in the 81st minute, although it was the Netherlands' only goal in a 3-1 loss. Nanninga had been a substitute in three previous World Cup matches, but failed to score.

ROBERTO ROJAS

THE PLAYER WHO was banned for life for faking an injury in a 1990 qualifying match.

Brazil led Chile 1-0 with 22 minutes remaining in a qualifying match in Rio de Janeiro on September 3, 1989, when Chilean goalkeeper Roberto Rojas fell backward and held his face in his hands just after a flare landed near him. The Chileans left the field and did not return, stating that their safety could not be ensured. Doctors examined Rojas and said he had a cut on his forehead, but no burns. The FIFA awarded the game to Brazil and eliminated Chile from the tournament. Rojas was banned for life for faking an injury.

171

HUNGARY

THE NATION THAT has reached the World Cup final twice, but has won only two final-round matches since 1966.

Hungary has an all-time World Cup record of 15 wins, 14 defeats, and three ties, and was runner-up in 1938 and 1954, but has had little success lately. The Hungarian national team qualified for the final round in 1934, 1938, 1954, 1958, 1962, 1966, 1978, 1982, and 1986. In their last three final-round appearances Hungary's final-round record has been only two wins, six losses, and a draw.

PERU

THE TEAM THAT played a World Cup match only two days after the country was devastated by an earthquake.

Peru opened play at the 1970 World Cup in Mexico on June 2 against Bulgaria in León only two days after Peru was devastated by an earthquake that claimed 66,794 lives. Bulgaria led 2-0 early in the second half, but Peru rallied to win 3-2.

ROSEMARY de MELLO

THE WOMAN WHO achieved commer-
cial success for throwing a flare at a World
Cup qualifying match.

Rosemary de Mello threw a flare onto the field at a
Brazil vs. Chile qualifying match in Rio de Janeiro on
September 3, 1989, which resulted in the game being
cut short with 22 minutes remaining. Afterward, she re-
ceived an offer from the Brazilian editor of *Playboy* to
pose for a centerfold and appeared in television com-
mercials. Known as "Rocket Rosey," she did one
TV ad for a travel agency announcing that she
was going to the World Cup the following
summer in Italy, but without her
fireworks.

GRZEGORZ LATO

THE LEADING SCORER in the 1974 World Cup.

Grzegorz Lato scored seven goals for Poland in 1974, the most by any player in that year's tournament, in leading his team to six wins in seven matches. Lato scored two in a 3-2 win over Argentina on June 15, two versus Haiti as Poland rolled 7-0 on June 19, beat Sweden 1-0 with a score on June 26, and added another on June 30 in a 2-1 triumph over Yugoslavia. In the third-place match against Brazil on July 6, Lato scored the game's only goal for a 1-0 victory. He is the only Polish player to lead all scorers in a tournament.

WEST GERMANY

THE COUNTRY THAT celebrated the 20th anniversary of its first World Cup victory by winning at home in 1974.

West Germany won the World Cup in 1954, then won again in 1974 in front of home fans in five West German cities. West Germany beat Chile 1-0 and beat Australia 3-0, but lost to East Germany 1-0, though the defeat did not prevent the West Germans from reaching the second round. There, West Germany won all three, 2-0 over Yugoslavia, 4-2 against Sweden, and 1-0 versus Poland. In the final, West Germany downed the Netherlands 2-1.

176

STEVE ADAMACHE

THE FIRST GOALKEEPER to be substi-
tuted for in a World Cup match.

Steve Adamache of Romania was the first goalkeeper to be taken out for a substitute in a World Cup
match. He was removed because of injury after 29 minutes on June 10, 1970, against Brazil, and replaced by
Necula Raducanu. Brazil won 3-2.

ITALY, 1950

THE TEAM WHOSE chances of winning three consecutive World Cups were lost in an airline disaster.

Italy won two World Cups before World War II, in 1934 and 1938, and was expected to field a strong team in the first postwar championship in 1950. The Italians were decimated, however, by the crash of the airplane carrying the Torino team on May 5, 1949, on the return from a match in Portugal. Every player was killed, including eight from the national team. The Torino team had won five consecutive Italian national championships. The 1950 Italian team lost 3-2 to Sweden and won 2-0 over Paraguay.

CONGO VS.
CAMEROON, 1978

THE QUALIFYING MATCH where paratroopers were sent to quell a riot.

Cameroon and the Congo met in a tense qualifying
match for the 1978 World Cup on October 31, 1976
in Yaoundé, Cameroon. The referee awarded a penalty
kick to Cameroon and was attacked by the Congolese
goalkeeper. A melee ensued, and Cameroon President
Ahmadou Ahidjo sent in paratroopers by helicopter to
quash the riot. The Congo won the match 2-1.

JEAN-MARIE PFAFF

THE GOALKEEPER WHO survived a near drowning and shut out his opponent on the same day.

Shortly before a match against El Salvador on June 19, 1982, in Elche, Spain, Jean-Marie Pfaff, Belgium's goalkeeper, nearly drowned in an accident at the team's hotel. Pfaff recovered sufficiently to help his squad shut down El Salvador and win 1-0. Four days later, El Salvador was shut out by Argentina 2-0. Belgium has not qualified for a final round since.

OTTORINO BARASSI

THE KEEPER OF the World Cup trophy for most of World War II.

Italy won title to the World Cup for four years after winning the championship in 1938, but ended up with it for 12 because of the intervention of World War II, which prevented a World Cup from being staged in 1942 or 1946. Ottorino Barassi, head of Italian Sport, feared the Nazis would confiscate the trophy, so for most of World War II, he kept the valued piece of hardware in a shoebox under his bed.

JOHAN NEESKENS

THE FIRST PLAYER to score a penalty kick in a World Cup final.

Johann Cruyff of the Netherlands was fouled by West Germany's Uli Hoeness in the penalty area in the first minute of the final on July 7, 1974, in Munich, setting up a penalty kick by Johan Neeskens to give the Netherlands a 1-0 lead. It was the first penalty kick ever in a World Cup final. The second came shortly. In the 26th minute, Paul Breitner of West Germany converted a penalty kick to tie the match 1-1. West Germany went on to win 2-1.

MARIO ZAGALO

THE ONLY INDIVIDUAL to play on two
World Cup champions and manage another.

Mario Zagalo played left wing for Brazil's World
Cup champions of 1958 and 1962 and scored a goal in
each tournament. In 1970, he was named team manager
as a last-minute replacement for João Saldanha, and led
Brazil to another title. Zagalo was credited with stabi-
lizing a Brazilian team disrupted by dissension.

PORTUGAL

THE NATION THAT has been in the final round only twice, but has claimed twice as many victories as defeats.

Portugal qualified for the final round of the World Cup for the first time in 1966 and, behind the brilliance of Eusébio, finished in third place. Unfortunately, Portugal was unable to build on that success. It has qualified only one other time, in 1986, when the Portuguese won once and lost twice. Overall, Portugal's record is six wins and three defeats.

UNITED STATES

THE 1930 TEAM nicknamed the "shot-putters."

The 1930 World Cup team from the U.S. was nicknamed the "shot-putters" by the French because of its unusually large and muscular players. Coached by Jack Coll, the squad was made up largely of foreign-born players, principally from England and Scotland. The U.S. reached the semifinals with a pair of 3-0 wins over Belgium and Paraguay. In the semis, the roof caved in, however, as the U.S. lost 6-1 to Argentina. The Argentines overpowered the Americans with five second-half goals, three of them scored in nine minutes.

ERNST JEAN-JOSEPH

THE FIRST WORLD Cup player to be
suspended by the FIFA for drug use.

Ernst Jean-Joseph of Haiti was the first player to be
suspended by the FIFA for drug use during the World
Cup. Under the procedure begun in 1966, the FIFA
checks two players from each team before and after each
game. Jean-Joseph was suspended on June 18, 1974, for
taking a stimulant containing phenylmetrazin.

ITALY AND BRAZIL

THE TWO NATIONS to win back-to-back World Cups.

West Germany (now just Germany) in 1994 will be attempting to become the third country to win consecutive World Cups. The only two to accomplish the feat are Italy in 1934 and 1938 and Brazil in 1958 and 1962.

EMILIO BUTRAGUEÑO

THE ONLY PLAYER since 1966 to score four goals in a World Cup match.

Nine players have scored four goals in a World Cup game, but Emilio Butragueño of Spain is the only one to accomplish the feat since 1966. It happened on June 18, 1986, in Spain's 5-1 win over Denmark in Querétaro, Mexico. It is also the only time in which Denmark has lost a final-round game. Prior to this match, Butragueño owned only one World Cup goal. After his four-goal explosion, he never found the net again in World Cup play.

BULGARIA

THE ONLY NATION to play more than
eight final-round games without a victory.

Bulgaria has qualified for the World Cup final
round in 1962, 1966, 1970, 1974, and 1986, but is
still looking for its first victory. In 16 matches, Bulgaria
has lost 10 and tied six and has been outscored 35-11.

ENGLAND VS. BRAZIL, 1958

THE FIRST SCORELESS draw in World Cup history.

Scoreless draws have become relatively common-place in recent World Cup play, but the first did not come until 1958, the sixth tournament. England and Brazil battled through a goalless 90 minutes on June 11 in Gothenburg, Sweden. Prior to that day, there had been 109 matches in the final round in World Cup history. There were a record seven scoreless draws in the 1982 tournament.

YUGOSLAVIA

THE ONLY TEAM to have seven different players score goals in one game.

An incredible seven different players scored for
Yugoslavia on June 18, 1974, in a 9-0 rout of Zaire in
Gelsenkirchen, West Germany. Dusan Bajević scored
three times, and Dragan Dzajić, Ivan Surjak, Josip
Katalinski, Vladimir Bogicević, Branko Oblak, and Ilja
Petković each scored once. Yugoslavia did not use a sin-
gle substitute in the match.

AUGUSTO AND RAMON CANALES

THE TWO BROTHERS hired by Peru to put a hex on opponents.

Augusto and Ramon Canales were retained by the Peruvians at the World Cup in 1982 to put a hex on opponents by means of special herbs, clay dolls, and magic rattles. They were unsuccessful. Peru tied Cameroon 0-0, tied Italy 1-1, and lost 5-1 to Poland in a match in which the Poles scored all of their goals in a 22-minute blitz in the second half.

WOLFGANG WEBER

THE PLAYER WHO kicked a game-tying goal with 15 seconds left in the 1966 World Cup final to force extra time.

England and West Germany met on July 30, 1966, in London to decide the eighth World Cup champion. West Germany scored first, but England answered with two goals for a 2-1 lead. A win for England seemed assured until Jack Charlton of England fouled Siggi Held. The free kick was worked into a goal by Wolfgang Weber with only 15 seconds remaining, forcing extra time. England overcame the disappointment to win 4-2 in extra time.

LEONEL SÁNCHEZ

THE PLAYER WHO threw a punch in
1962 that was seen by millions on TV but
was missed by the officials.

In a brutal match between Chile and Italy in Santiago
on June 2, 1962, two players were ejected and the referee was injured. Giorgio Ferrini of Italy was red-carded
for fighting, but refused to leave the field and had to be
removed by the police. Leonel Sánchez of Chile, the son
of a professional boxer, broke the nose of Humberto
Maschio of Italy with a roundhouse punch that was
clearly seen by millions on television, but went
unpunished, because it was missed by a
linesman standing a few feet away.
Chile won 2-0.

EGYPT AND ZAIRE

THE TWO NATIONS involved in the
great "monkey meat" controversy of 1974.

Zaire reached the final round of the World Cup for
the only time in its history in 1974. In March for a
preparatory match against Egypt's national team in
Alexandria, cooks at the Zaire team's hotel protested
when they were asked to cook the visitors' national
dish—monkeys brought from Zaire skinned and
dressed. Hotel management agreed to allow the players to prepare their own meals, provided they
dined in their rooms.

PATRICK BATTISTON

THE FRENCH PLAYER who was severely injured by a goalkeeper in the 1982 World Cup.

Patrick Battiston of France was racing toward the West German goal in the semifinal on July 8, 1982, when he was severely injured by West German goalkeeper Harald Schumacher. Schumacher smashed Battiston to the ground, leaving the Frenchman unconscious for three minutes and with injuries that sidelined him for six months. Schumacher was not penalized. West Germany won 5-4 on penalties.

UNITED STATES

THE TEAM THAT lost a semifinal by
five goals and its trainer to the contents from
his medical bag.

The United States was blitzed by Argentina 6-1 in the
semifinals of the World Cup on July 26, 1930, in
Montevideo, Uruguay, and if that were not bad enough,
the American trainer had to be carried off the field. The
trainer, displeased when the referee gave a free kick to
Argentina, dashed onto the field to protest. He threw
his medical supplies to the ground to emphasize
his point, which broke open a chloroform bot-
tle. The fumes knocked the trainer out
cold.

BELGIUM

THE ONLY TEAM to fail to reach the final round despite being unscored upon in the qualifying round.

Only one team was slated to qualify from Europe group three in 1974, consisting of teams from Belgium, Iceland, Norway, and the Netherlands. Despite outscoring the opposition 12-0 in four wins and two draws, Belgium finished second to the Netherlands on goal difference. The Netherlands also had four wins and two draws, but outscored opponents in the group by 24-2. The two matches between the Netherlands and Belgium resulted in scoreless draws.

CZECHOSLOVAKIA AND BRAZIL

THE TWO NATIONS that participated in the vicious "Battle of Bordeaux."

The match between Czechoslovakia and Brazil on June 12, 1938, in Bordeaux, France, is one of the most vicious international matches on record. Three players were ejected, and three Czechs suffered devastating injuries. The game ended in a 1-1 tie. Two days later, the two teams met in a replay, but 15 of the 22 players who played in the previous match were unable to participate because of injuries. Brazil won the replay 2-1 in a cleanly played anticlimax.

199

CUBA

THE ONLY NATION whose last World Cup final-round win came before World War II.

Cuba qualified for the final round only in 1938. In the first game, the Cubans tied Romania 3-3 on June 5 in Toulouse, France. In a replay four days later, they defeated the Romanians 2-1 despite switching goalkeepers. Cuba bowed out of the tournament on June 12 when it was thrashed 8-0 by Sweden in Antibes.

SOVIET UNION

THE NATION THAT earned 36 points in World Cup competition, but failed to win a title.

The Soviet Union is seventh in the all-time World Cup standings with 36 points on 15 victories and six draws in 31 matches. The top six all have championships, however. The Soviet Union's best finish was fourth place in 1966. The nation has not been able to duplicate its success with soccer that it has in several other sports. The breakup of the former USSR makes the future unpredictable. In the 1994 qualifying round, teams from Russia, Estonia, Latvia, and Lithuania in the former Soviet Union will compete.

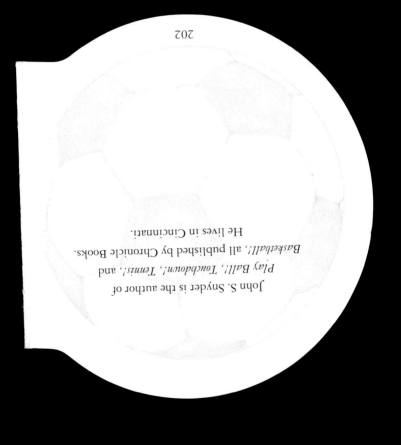

John S. Snyder is the author of
Play Ball!, *Touchdown!*, *Tennis!*, and
Basketball!, all published by Chronicle Books.
He lives in Cincinnati.